SHOESTRING EMPIRE

ASHLEY ELKINS

Copyright ©2023, Ashley Elkins

All rights reserved. No part of this publication may be reproduced, distributed, or transmitted in any form or by any means, including photocopying, recording, or other electronic or mechanical methods, without the prior written permission of the publisher, except in the case of brief quotations embodied in reviews and specific other non-commercial uses permitted by copyright law.

ISBN: 979-8-88759-735-5 - paperback
ISBN: 979-8-88759-736-2 - ebook

This book is dedicated to my precious husband, Chris, who somehow believes in me always. And to my wonderful daughters, Vivienne and Layla, who give me the motivation to go and do great things. Thank you for your support; I am forever thankful for you.

Table of Contents

Welcome
Introduction: You Can Do This 7

Before You Begin
Chapter 1: Borrowing Confidence 11
Chapter 2: What Do You Have? 19
Chapter 3: What Do You Need? 27
Chapter 4: Making a Way 33

Getting Started
Chapter 5: Branding. 39
Chapter 6: Listings. 45
Chapter 7: Social Media 49
Chapter 8: Next Steps 59
Chapter 9: Legal Advice. 65
Chapter 10: Mental Readiness 73

Go! Go! Go!
Chapter 11: Borrowing Credibility. 79
Chapter 12: Smarter and Harder 83
Chapter 13: When to Spend. 89
Chapter 14: Lean, not Cheap. 97
Chapter 15: Free Resources 103

Scale It Up
Chapter 16: Marketing. 109
Chapter 17: Growing 117

You Can Do It
Chapter 18: Worth it all 123
Note to reader 127
Sources. 128

Welcome

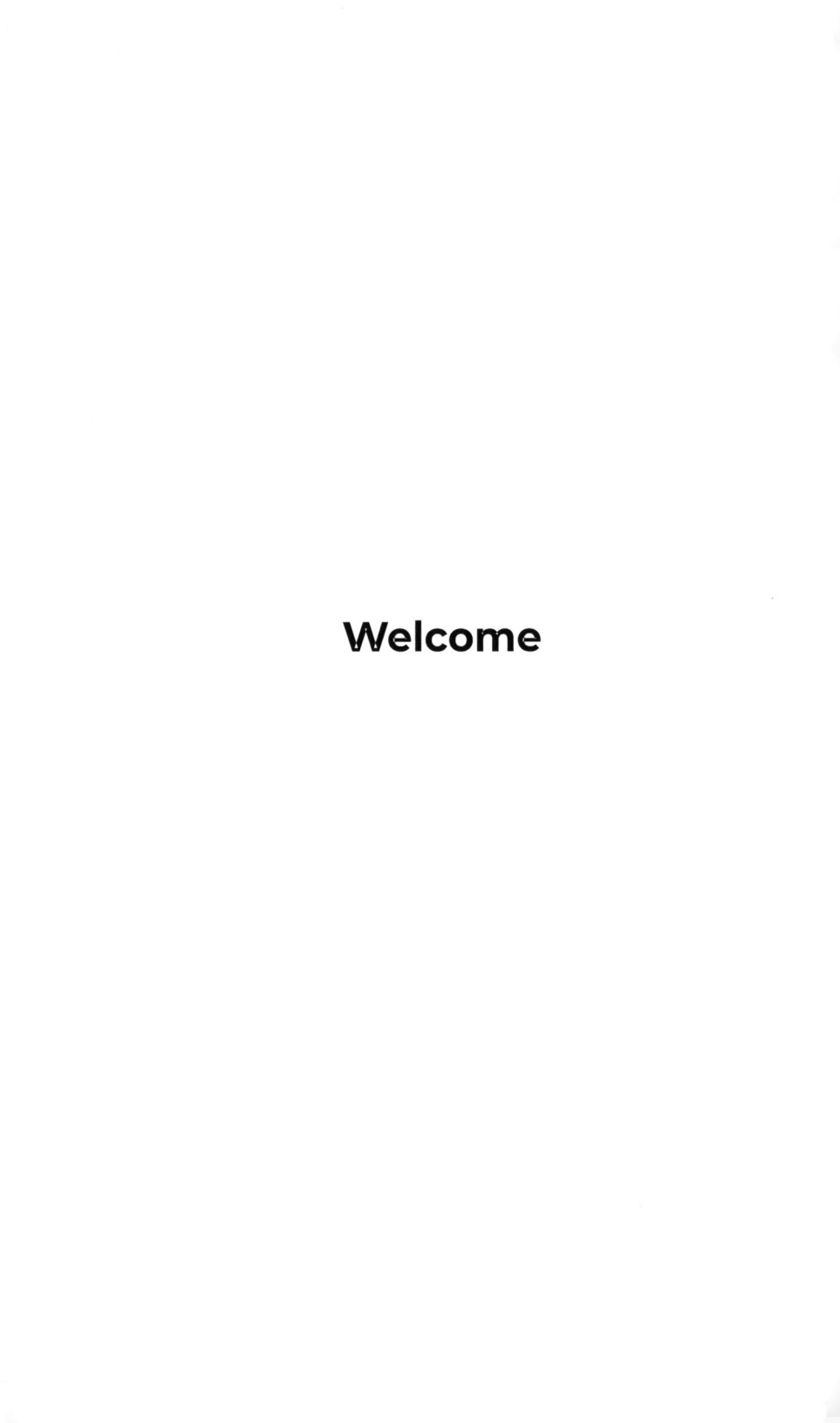

Introduction
You Can Do This

If I know one person who wants to become an entrepreneur, I know a hundred.

We talk about their wonderful ideas. They often have very specific plans about what they would do and how. They also have no shortage of inspiration to start their side hustle or finally leave a soul-draining job and strike out on their own.

But there's a holdup: They don't think they have enough money to pull the trigger and launch their dreams.

I know better. Many businesses can be established with relatively small initial investments. Most potential business owners I know actually have the resources they need. They just don't know it.

This book is called *Shoestring Empire* because it's shocking how little capital you need to get your business up and going.

Several years ago, I took a leap of faith and started my own marketing agency. That was a scary thing to do. It also turned out to be a great blessing.

Shakespeare said, "Uneasy lies the head that wears the crown," but Mel Brooks said, "It's good to be the king." I'm happy to be the queen or boss if you prefer. The tradeoffs are so completely worth it for me. And over the course of building my little empire, I've helped other people start and grow their own businesses. That provided a unique perspective that inspired this book.

Since marketing is my business, I understand how to get the word out. However, this isn't a marketing book. It's about helping you pull the trigger on your own idea and launch that dream you've nurtured for so long.

I started with next to nothing. My company, Vitality South, isn't as big as I want it to be. We're still growing and learning, but there's no doubt my leap of faith has paid off for me and my family. Along the way, I've learned quite a bit about what it takes to get a business up and running on a limited budget.

Let me be clear: There are plenty of legitimate reasons not to start your business now, but a small budget isn't one of them.

If that's what's holding you back, I want to eliminate your concerns. I want this book to be the pep talk that pushes you off the fence and gets you going. I also want it to be a practical guide filled with nuts-and-bolts tips you can use as you work toward your entrepreneurial dreams.

My overall message is as straightforward as can be: I started my business on a shoestring budget, and so can you. It won't be easy, but it could be magnificent.

Before You Begin

Chapter 1
Borrowing Confidence

I had wanted to start a business for years but lacked the confidence to make the first move. I had the skills to do the work. I also had the knowledge to help my customers and the experience to earn their trust.

Still, I hesitated. I didn't dare jump over the ledge to pursue my dream.

Instead, I stayed where I was. I focused on doing good work for the company. Though the pay wasn't what I deserved, I took some comfort in the knowledge that I was helping my customers.

The comfort didn't last. Giving your all to a company that doesn't give back starts to hurt after a while. Big accomplishments deserve big rewards. But whenever I closed a deal that put money in the company's coffers, I went back to work without words of thanks or promises of higher pay.

Incredibly tired, I would sit at my desk and ask, "Why am I going so hard?"

My customers had no idea what I was going through and neither did my co-workers, but I knew. I eventually reached the point where the pain of staying was worse than the fear of the unknown.

Look, I've got nothing against working for somebody else. A good job can provide stability, security, and satisfaction.

However, the relationship between you and your employer has to be a two-way street. You need to receive as much from your job as you put into it. The give-and-take ebbs and flows from time to time, but bosses are responsible for taking care of their employees. If they don't, they've got no reason to complain when those employees pack up their offices and leave.

Why didn't I jump sooner?

I was afraid:

- of failing
- of losing my business investment
- of being unemployed
- of the unknowns
- of letting others down
- of bruising my ego

I could probably go on like this for the entire book. There were so many things that scared me before I took the plunge, but I think author Susan Jeffers had it right when she said, "Feel the fear and do it anyway." That's the spirit of courage I embraced and still do to this day.

One reason people don't move forward is they don't think they know everything about their industry. They don't want a potential customer to ask a question that they can't answer. They also don't want to try to sell themselves as experts on things they haven't dealt with yet.

That kind of thinking can lead you to paralysis by analysis. You think forever instead of taking action in the direction of your dreams. But the truth is you'll never know everything about your industry. It's impossible. If you really think about it, that excuse falls apart under its own weight.

A few years ago, my daughter played soccer. My husband grew up playing soccer, so he volunteered to coach her team. A couple of years later, my youngest daughter was old enough to play, and she asked me to be her coach. I agreed. It was only fair. Except for this one little truth: Not only had I never played soccer, but I had never watched a game. I definitely didn't know the rules.

But I was an excellent coach for that team of 4-year-olds. I researched the rules, looked up some best practices and drills, and made it fun. I didn't have to know everything about soccer. My job was to make sure I knew just a little more than a bunch of kids, which, really, wasn't that difficult.

You don't have to know everything about your field either. It's okay to say, "I don't know. Let me research that for you." This is growth. Don't fear it. Embrace it.

When people first accept a role of authority on a subject matter, they can have imposter syndrome. They feel as if they are not wise enough to deserve the titles and positions of authority that they assume. They blindly accept the advice of friends and reviews from strangers. They seek answers from online blog writers who may, or may not, know which way is up.

In addition, they can get a type of stage fright when put in the spotlight. They can momentarily forget what knowledge they actually do possess.

The only answer is to take a few deep breaths and remember the real truth: Nobody knows everything. If you know more than the people you're assisting, that's enough even if you have to go learn it to stay a step ahead. You are enough.

Even when you have all the knowledge you need, it's still a big mental shift to actually go forward into the unknown of owning and running your own business. When I told a friend how incredibly unhappy I was at my previous job but how much I loved my profession, he asked me why I didn't start my own business. It took my breath away.

I was talking about finding a different job and working for someone else. When he suggested that I start my own business, he also shared his confidence that I could do it. It made me realize how foolish all my fears were, and then, suddenly, I knew I could do it.

The crazy thing was my husband and family had been saying the same thing for years, but I'd assumed they were biased by their great and overwhelming love for me. I thought they were too confident in my abilities, and I suspected they were saying all those nice things to be, well, nice.

But when someone outside of my family saw my true potential, I finally recognized my opportunity. He had the confidence that I could do it, and I realized something important that's made a world of difference in my life.

I borrowed his confidence.

When he and I had that conversation, it was a chance encounter. I didn't orchestrate it or make it happen. He was a professional friend, so we didn't hang out on the weekends, but he had immeasurable business acumen that I respected immensely. His faith in me supercharged my own. I knew I had to take the first step.

Would it have been better if I hadn't had to borrow his confidence in me? Maybe. But who's to say? In business and in life, we all need quality advice from time to time. His words of support came exactly when I needed them and pushed me toward opportunities I hadn't thought I was ready to seize.

When I told my family and friends what he'd said, they all wondered what had taken me so long to get the message. For whatever reason and with a pocketful of borrowed confidence, I was ready to go. I was on fire and couldn't NOT do it.

However, there was a problem.

Because this was a great and sudden awakening for me, I had not been saving, scrimping, planning, or scheming. From the day I decided I wanted to move forward to the day I was sitting in my new office was less than a month. Not everyone can or should move that quickly. Yet others may be able to move even faster than that. When I realized I was ready to start, I had to quickly figure out how to make it happen. I am not a trust-fund baby, so I had to get creative. Luckily for me, that's one of my strengths.

If you are wanting to get started but are afraid you don't have what it takes, don't wait around like I did, hoping for someone to tell you what you should do. Carpe diem is the Latin phrase for "seize the day." Believe in yourself and move forward.

It doesn't take incredible intelligence to start a successful business. If you have the idea and the gumption, you can figure out the rest.

And if you don't have the confidence you need, borrow it. Find a friend or relative or business acquaintance who believes in you. Confide in that person and share your hopes and dreams. Ask them if they believe you have what it takes.

The point of this is not to give away your rights or demand permission to start your new business. It's simply a way to find the confidence you need to proceed. If, like me, you don't have that confidence, borrow it from someone you trust.

Here's a key point: Even if your confidence is borrowed, you need to own it.

The person looking at you in the mirror every morning is the person you'll face when times get hard. You are the person who has to keep going when you get tired. Your inner voice is the one you'll need to trust from sun up to sundown. As Shakespeare wrote, "Screw your courage to the sticking place," so it's there when you need it.

You can do this. You need to know that in your bones. It won't be easy, but nothing worth doing ever is. Once you have the courage to say out loud, "I am going to be a successful business owner," and mean it, you're more than halfway there.

Figure out the rest along the way.

Chapter 2
What Do You Have?

I could stand in my garage all day and say that I'm a car and believe it, but that doesn't make me a car. Saying that you're a successful business owner is an important mindset, but it needs to be followed by a whole bunch of action on your part. Thinking's all well and good, but you've got to do things.

Once you've made up your mind and said, "Yes, I will move forward," you need to figure out how to do it without breaking the bank. You'll want to start by taking a hard look at resources you have on hand or could easily and inexpensively get.

Money in the bank is great, but if you're reading this, it's probably because you're somewhat shy of the billion dollars you'd like to have. For now, we'll assume money is something you're more interested in making than spending.

Before we go forward, I encourage you to pause to get a notebook and a pencil. The hope is this book will provide practical steps while also sparking your creativity. Writing things down lets you know exactly where you stand and provides a place to capture your own thoughts and intuitions about how to navigate the road ahead. You can visit https://shoestringempire.com to download a free workbook to use for planning your business, or plain paper works too. Jot down anything that occurs to you, even if it feels small or silly at first. You don't have to show this list to anyone. This list can include competencies, connections, your cryptocurrency portfolio — whatever you have.

Some non-monetary resources might not initially occur to you. Ask yourself these questions:

- Do I have an active social media account with many connections?
- Do I have a long list of email addresses that I *have permission* to email?
- Do I have a talent for public speaking? A knack for writing?
- Do I serve on a board that is filled with the exact kind of people that would make excellent customers or advocates for my products/services?
- Do I have friends who owe me favors?
- Do I have a great mentor?
- Do I have good credit?

All of these things matter. Once you fully catalog the list of your resources, it's a good idea to make a second list of resources that you don't have but that could help you along the way.

Start with the list of questions you just read. If you said, "No," to any of them, start there. It's impossible for me to know exactly what your needs are, so I can't provide a complete list of what you will find useful. But you are more than capable of creating such a list.

That's right: I'm asking you to brainstorm. Get your pen or pencil going. Pile up as many ideas as you can dream up, and don't judge them because a bad idea can often point to a good one.

Be sure to include how much money you think you will need for at least the first six months of operations and any non-optional equipment or purchases to get your business started. You know your profession. Feel free to be as lofty as you wish. Don't limit yourself to what you think is easily achieved. If it's worthwhile, it may be worth the challenge.

I guess I should have warned you before that I'm a list maker. But if you're going to be strategic and get stuff done, you need to have written goals and plans.

Sorry, not sorry.

If you haven't stopped at this point and made your list, hit the brakes. Moving on without making this list is like sitting on your couch eating a donut while watching exercise tapes on TV. That's not going to cut it. If you're investing your time and resources into reading this book, you want to get the most out of it. Your participation is crucial because, after all, it's your business.

When we examine our first list of current assets, we need to decide how we can best take advantage of them. We can't be willy-nilly about how we use our current resources even if they are non-monetary:

- If you listed a thriving social media network, how can you turn those friends/followers into customers or advocates?
- If you listed writing as a strength, what and where can you write to help jumpstart your business?
- If you are a great public speaker, what platforms can give you the most exposure to your target audience?

I'm sure you've heard that writing down your idea makes it a goal while adding steps and deadlines makes it a plan. If you leave these ideas on paper, you have a bunch of writing. If you treat them like action items, you start building a business.

So look at your ideas and turn them into plans. If you said an active social media following is a resource of yours, consider creating a social media page for your new business. Invite all of your friends to follow the page, and commit to posting to it at least 3 times per week. Reach out to your close circle and ask them if they will invite their friends.

At my company, we post three times a week for one of my customers. One post is a product (or service) post telling more about the offering, one is a tip post that helps the audience learn something, and one is a behind-the-scenes post to make your audience feel connected.

That's a great, all-purpose model, and three times per week is very doable. You can easily hold yourself accountable now that you have a plan.

If your goal is to find a mentor, set a deadline for making a short list of who you'd like your mentor to be. After that, set another deadline to reach out to that person. You can only control what you can control. You can't make people or businesses respond or take action, but you can be responsible for your actions.

Here I go again: I can't stress enough how important it is that you spend some time and effort fleshing out your list of current resources and coming up with ways to get the most out of them.

Engage with this process.

It's your future.

So make your lists and spend time thinking about everything you wrote down. It's important to treat your lists as living documents. It's not a one-and-done kind of thing. If you're serious about going forward, ideas will come to you while mowing the grass, walking the dog, or taking a shower. Get used to writing them down. Ideas are fleeting. Catch them so you can use them. If you have a smartphone, use the Notes app. Siri is good about capturing ideas and storing them for later.

The more brainstorming you do, the more answers you have to the question, "What should I do now?"

As you look at your list of opportunities, begin thinking about how you can develop "wants" into "haves." Start asking questions:

- What is the lowest-hanging fruit?
- What would be the most impactful for me and my new business?

These days, consumers spend billions of dollars on products and services they discover through social media, but it isn't for everybody. If your business isn't based online, don't start with the social media opportunity.

But if you have social media skills, start thinking of ways to be strategic about it. WHICH social media channel should you pursue?

I'll get further into the social media for businesses in Chapter 7, so I'm not going to work through that at this point. Remember, the more specific you can get on your goals, the less daunting it will feel when it's time to implement your plan.

Personally, I like to get out some highlighters or colored pens and go through my list highlighting/ranking the highest priorities based on ease and impact. I prefer to do easy things that achieve maximum benefit for my business. They're the absolute best. And I ignore the things that seem insurmountable and wouldn't do much in the way of pushing my business forward.

What about the middle bits, the ideas that take some work and help in some ways? That's where art and science mix with business. You'll have to use your good judgment and experiment with what works.

When this exercise is finished, you should have a pretty good idea of what you have in your toolbox. One way to add to your collection of tools is to invest your money in smart ways. Just because this book focuses on doing the most with the least startup capital doesn't mean your time is worthless. Consider if your time would be better served purchasing what you need, so you can focus on other areas.

I've learned over the years that I can earn the money to pay my bookkeeper more quickly than I can manage my own books. For me, the expense is well worth the money.

Here's another example: Let's say you wanted a mentor, but no one comes to mind. You could research who would be a good fit, stalk that person to find contact information, keep reaching out until the person gives in, and celebrate the relationship with a new mentor.

Or you could hire a business coach.

Both approaches work. As I hope you're beginning to recognize, it's always a matter of priorities.

Chapter 3

What Do You Need?

Even on a shoestring, you'll need money to launch your passion project. The amount depends on your dreams, but as the old adage goes, "You have to spend money to make money."

So let's look at ways to get the cash you need.

In addition to using your credit, savings, and loans, which all have a time and place, there are other ways to raise the capital needed to turn your dream into a reality. Some of your options include grants, crowdfunding, bartering, and start-up revenue generation. These types of opportunities are only available to the resourceful and persistent. Luckily, you can be both if you set your mind to it.

Grants are a fun world to explore. There are opportunities everywhere if you can tap into that resource. The beautiful thing about grants is that you typically don't have to pay them back.

On the front end, you need to find the grant, apply for it, and make sure you meet your end of the deal. What you're looking for in grants is free money that allows you to do what you already wanted to do in the first place.

You don't want grants to be a side hustle or distraction. Before you apply, make sure it will provide extra financial support while you keep the main thing the main thing.

To find a grant, I recommend starting with grant.gov. To register for an account, you'll have to have a non-proprietary identifier that is provided by the System for Award Management (SAM.gov). It'll probably take a few weeks to sign up for this, so plan accordingly.

On grants.gov, you can filter by the specifics of what you do and your business identity to narrow your search for grants that fit you and your business.

The trick to writing a grant is to put yourself in the shoes of the decision maker and tailor your application to what they're looking for. For example, if it's a grant for furthering art education in children, and that's part of your mission, make sure your purpose for seeking the grant is to further art education for children in your unique way.

Consider buying a subscription to grantwatch.com, which will save you time and keep you aware of what's available. In addition, connecting with other organizations and entities can open up grant opportunities.

Now, our search for resources goes old-school. Think about harnessing the power of the barter system.

I'm talking about the olden days of trading a dozen eggs for a loaf of bread. This can be done with products or services.

The key here is to make sure both sides of the bargain are getting something they need.

If you have a gymnastics studio, you could trade a gift certificate for a year's worth of your classes to a bookkeeper, who has a daughter that would like to take gymnastics classes. The exchange is a good deal for both of you. If all goes well, this barter could continue profiting the gym and bookkeeper for years to come. The power of the barter is a great resource for your toolbox.

Crowdfunding is another modern alternative to traditional loans. I'm sure you've heard of platforms like gofundme.org. In it, you can ask others, likely strangers, to invest in your business. You can promise them returns, such as

- t-shirts
- a first release when the product launches
- their name listed in the credits
- whatever creative idea you come up with

You can scale the benefits based on the level of contribution. There are other organizations with similar models, so do your research to determine which solution works best for you.

If you'd rather have locals than strangers help crowdsource your business, you could start off with a pre-sale to raise the necessary capital. Gift cards are a traditional pay-first-enjoy-later model. You could offer a discount to get as much paid-upfront revenue as possible.

If you are a landscaper, you could offer a package in which you cut grass X number of times for a flat rate with a discount to encourage payment upfront. Traditionally, 20 percent is the lowest number that will entice action, but this number will vary greatly from industry to industry.

Also on the local side of things, remember the people who encouraged you to start your business. Some of them might be willing to offer you a low-cost loan to help you get started.

If you're looking for a traditional loan, banks have vaults filled with money. I've found that smaller community banks are friendlier to people who don't have a particularly long credit history, especially if you have a relationship built with them.

If you have been turned down by a regular bank, there may still be an opportunity for a loan. I am not an expert on banking, so I spoke with a couple of executives in the commercial lending division at my local non-profit Community Development Financial Institution.

I was delighted to hear that they often lend to new and existing businesses that traditional banks are unable to assist. There are non-profit CDFIs throughout the United States. Not only are they able to say, "Yes," more often than other lending institutions, but they also offer free business coaching so that the businesses they serve are more likely to succeed.

Options are everywhere for funding possibilities. The list of opportunities includes

- loans
- credit
- bartering
- crowdfunding
- pre-sales
- grants

I'm sure if you think about it, you can discover different funding options available to you. When you are deciding how much money you need for your business, it's usually more than you first think. Not only will you need start-up capital but also operating capital to keep you going as expenses arise. Find which route, or routes, will work best for your business and pursue them with all due diligence.

Chapter 4
Making a Way

I was talking with someone who owns a business while she and her husband are both employed elsewhere full-time. She wanted so badly to be a full-time business owner and quit her 9-to-5. She couldn't afford to quit her job because she has too many bills. She said she needed that paycheck.

I guided her through an exercise to prepare for the day when she could step away from her job and live her dream. She left our meeting with a concrete plan.

You knew it was coming: Note-taking time. If you're in her situation, get out a piece of paper and a pen, and let's examine your obligations.

If you have already quit your full-time business, feel free to skip this entire chapter. It's focused on figuring out if and when you can take that step.

To get started, I encourage you to pull up your bank account. Make a list of all of your current bills. It can include necessary things like a mortgage or luxury things like a Fruit-of-the-Month club. Beside each, note that it's a monthly financial obligation. Let this list rest here for a minute. We'll come back to it.

The next thing you need to consider is how much of your paycheck you need to replace before you can go full-time. You know the dollar amount that you're earning from your job, but that doesn't always match the number you need to replace the income:

- What if you got a demotion or fewer hours at work?
- What if your paycheck were $100 less per month?
- How about $200?
- $1000?
- Could you survive?

I don't know your number, but even if you can't replace your entire paycheck, will you still be able to pay all that's important?

Here's another question: If you give up your job, what other benefits might you lose? Benefits beyond the paycheck are important to consider.

Health insurance is a big one. If you lost your health insurance through your employer, how much would it cost to replace it? This varies from company to company in how much they contribute to your plan. Actually do the research on this one.

I found for my family, the Health Exchange coverage and the price was comparable to what my previous employer had provided, but you'll have to discover for yourself. I've also consulted with people who found the Health Exchange more affordable and some that did not. I am not an insurance representative and do not know the needs of your family, so you owe it to yourself to do your own research.

Besides the loss of insurance, consider what other benefits you'll lose if you quit your day job:

- Do they offer daycare?
- Do they provide your meals?
- A retirement match?
- Onsite medical clinic?

I know these sound lofty compared to the majority of employers, but if there are perks that benefit you, you need to figure out what their loss will mean to you financially. You want as complete an accounting as possible so you know the actual cost of replacing your paycheck.

You're looking at all the pluses and minuses, so you can make an informed decision. Once you know exactly how much of a monthly paycheck you need to replace, you start taking action by

- eliminating monthly recurring payments
- increasing revenue to make up for this difference

I don't pretend that budgeting is fun or easy, but if it's what's standing between you and your dream business, it's worth the time and effort.

Pull out the list of your monthly obligations and see what you can slash. How drastic you are will depend on how badly and quickly you want this to work. I can't make these decisions for you. I won't be sitting in your living room with you in the evenings with no Netflix.

As you work through this list, some things will be easy to eliminate. Most people stop there. If that's all you're willing to trim from your budget, that's okay. Trim that, put it in a savings account, and one day you can have enough to make this move. Or you could invest it in your business until you're making enough revenue to pay your salary and make that switch.

You don't have to go further than this, but let's look at some of the harder decisions you could make. These are "non-optional" obligations that can be made optional. One of the commitments on the list of the person I was consulting was a car payment that looked similar to a small mortgage.

I asked if she really needed that particular vehicle. She said it was 80 percent paid for, which is nice, but that also meant one to two more years of payments. At the time, used cars were selling at a premium. Could she sell it and buy outright a less expensive used car? She said not only could she sell it, but there was an extra truck at her house she could switch to. Not only could she eliminate the monthly payment, but she could get a chunk of cash to pay off her other obligations.

With her experience in mind, finish going through the list in its entirety to find any other opportunities. How close can you get to your goal?

You don't have to pretend that it's fun to sell a car you love. Maybe there is another way. Bringing in new income is far easier than eliminating debt. But cutting costs has been an important step for many business owners.

If there is a secret to success, it's about making commitments to yourself and keeping them. Olympian Peter Vidmar once said, "Don't sacrifice what you want most for what you want now. Write down what you want most and see it often." That quote is especially relevant if you're trying to build a *Shoestring Empire*.

The reasons many people want their own business is to become wealthy or to be their own boss. When I suggest giving up your prized possessions, it feels like the wrong direction. I get it. I've done it. It sucks. If those prized possessions are what you want most, this is a terrible plan for you. But if they are what's separating you from your dreams, seriously consider letting them go.

And remember, a successful business can buy them all back and then some.

What do you want most?

Getting Started

Chapter 5
Branding

To turn your idea into a business, you need to develop its brand. Branding is a huge concept that I could literally write an entire book about. Branding is essentially your business identity. That includes your business name, logo, color scheme, and personality. As we dive into each of these aspects, we'll discuss what's important to consider and the pitfalls to avoid.

Making good decisions now means there will be less to fix later in the game. It's so much easier to invest the early effort into getting things right than to pay the piper for our mistakes down the road.

When deciding upon your company's name, you'll want it to be something you're proud to say when you walk into a room full of important people. The rule of thumb from a marketing perspective is it needs to be easy to say, easy to read, and easy to remember. The test I've used again and again is the grandma test:

- Can she read it?
- Can she say it?
- Can she remember it?

If not, try again. Either your name or your tagline needs to let people know what you do. It's really hard and expensive to change your name down the road. It's not so much a legal issue as a practical one. If you have trucks with your name painted on the side and have invested in marketing your brand, a name change means you're starting nearly from scratch to rebuild brand awareness.

The next thing to consider is domain name availability. To make sure we're on the same page and I'm not talking too nerdy, a domain name is your website address, www.yourbusinessname.com. This may not be a priority for everyone, but if your business relies on a web presence and online traffic, it is paramount.

My business is about helping our customers navigate to stand out in the online, digital world. It was super important to find a great ".com" to accurately and effectively represent us online. We probably went through a hundred different business names until we found one where we got the .com for it.

A domain name usually costs $12 to $16 per year, which usually can be squeezed into the tightest of budgets. You can Google the domain name registry and find a plethora of websites that sell domain names.

Even though a domain name is cheap, remember that it's like real estate: Once it's gone, it's gone. As long as you pay your annual renewal, it's forever yours. Some people buy up names to resell at a profit. If you find one you want, buy it when you see it. Don't give your competition the chance to snatch up your domain name, so it points to their website instead of yours. If a great domain name is important to your business, plan it on the front end.

Another thing that readily comes to mind when you say "brand" is the logo. Logo design is the visual representation of the company:

- For McDonald's, it's the golden arches.
- For Nike, it's the swoosh.

Some people don't have specific emblems. They stand out by the way their names are written and the use of color. When starting a business on a shoestring budget, some decide to skip having a logo designed. While not technically a necessity, I think it really makes your business stand out and helps with marketing.

If you want a logo but don't have the budget to have one professionally designed, you can find a buddy with a kid in art school who will do it on the cheap. There are click-and-drag logo maker websites online you can use for free. Or there are websites online where you can contract with freelancers to do this for less money than a marketing agency will typically charge.

A lot of times, you get what you pay for. It ranges from a free, make-it-yourself price, to around $125 for freelancers from around the world, and probably starts around $500 up to thousands at professional design firms. But you can make the judgment call on what level of logo is best for you.

As far as the color scheme, you really get to make a judgment call here:

- Some business owners choose their favorite color.
- Some choose something that represents the products/services.
- Some look at the demographic they hope to serve and make a calculated guess at which colors most appeal to them.
- Some want something loud that will catch attention.

None of these methods is wrong. I would aim to be different from your closest competitors and choose something that won't alienate your ideal customers. You can even research what the colors mean and how those colors make customers feel. For this one, you really can let the spirit lead you. If you are working with a marketing agency, they are usually happy to help guide you on this choice.

Your personality sets the tone for your business. Are you formal or informal? Inclusive or exclusive? Conservative or colorful? This varies depending on the nature of the business and the personality of the business owner.

My recommendation would be to think about your ideal customer:

- Who are they?
- What do they look like?
- Where do they eat dinner?
- Where do they shop?

Once you get a good feel for who they are, then decide what tone would most appeal to them. Some types of businesses have less of a choice than others. I can't imagine a funeral home that is snarky and makes jokes to be successful. But who am I to judge? I'm sure there is a business out there making it work.

I know of a plumber who adds humor to their messages to make them stand apart. Nationwide, most of us are familiar with Wendy's on Twitter roasting people. I'm sure that's made them a lot of money by keeping the burger chain top of customers' minds. Find something that works for you and your ideal customer, and stick with it.

The entire idea of branding is to make your business stand out and be recognized. That means that once you have an identity, you'll need to use it consistently. So take the time to make sure you like your branding and aren't taking a good-enough-for-now approach. Branding is typically refreshed every three to five years, so don't pick something you won't want to live with for at least that long.

Take the time to visualize your ideal customer and work backward to determine how to get them to invest in your product or service. The sooner you can have people seeking you out, the less you'll have to spend on marketing in the long run.

Chapter 6
Listings

In my opinion as a veteran marketer and business owner, the first marketing move you should make is to get your business listed online.

Branding is also in the marketing universe, but what I am referring to now is an attempt to push your business out into the world and let others find it. Yes, there could be such a business that exists in which you don't want people finding out about your business online, calling you, and asking to be your customer, but those are few and far between. For the other 99 percent of the world, let's talk about listings.

The good thing to know about listings is that they are mostly free. Listings are the online equivalent of what the phone book used to mean for America. When someone looks up a business online, will they find you and your correct information? Some businesses, even when you look for them by name, are almost impossible to find. You can remedy that in just a few minutes by signing up for a business listing.

To sign up for a business listing, you need as much information as possible about your business. You can definitely update it later, but you don't want to put incorrect information out there. The way business listings work is they all look at the others, scrape that information, and then update their information with what they find elsewhere. Wrong information feels like a weed with a wide root system that you can never seem to get rid of, so it's best to set it up correctly the first time.

The reason we went through the branding exercise first is that you need all of that information for your listings. Use your business name, target audience, and tone when writing a description to attract your ideal customers. Include your logo in your profile as well as your phone number and address. You'll also want to add store hours, services, products, and anything else specific and important about your business.

We're not going to dive into Search Engine Optimization (SEO) in this book. That's a service that I offer my clients, but it's not necessarily cheap or easy. What we will do is set you up, so that when your business is ready to take that next step, you're in good shape.

I mention this here and now because business listings are a very important part of SEO. It's imperative that you list your name, address, and phone number exactly the same way every time you list it. Although search engines are good at parsing and using information, they are just computer programs and won't always realize variations of your business name or address are referring to the same entity. If your address is South Main Street, let's stick with one spelling. Switching among variations, such as S. Main St, South Main St., or S Main Street, is tempting fate. Pick one and be consistent with your digital presence. The same goes for your business name.

Now that we know how to set up your business listings, let's discuss where. As you could probably guess, Google is the king as far as search engines and listings. At the time I'm writing this, Google has approximately 70 percent market share in search. And the other search engines share the remaining 30 percent. For the biggest return on your time, make sure you list your business on Google.

To set up your Google Business Listing, you have to have a Google account. If you don't have one, you can set it up for free. If you have a Gmail email account, you already have one and can use that account.

Go to https://business.google.com. Fill it out as completely as possible. Take your time crafting your business description, making sure you describe your core services or products with words that people would use when searching. For example, if your business is a restaurant named Boogie's and you call your hamburgers "hamboogies," that may be cute and all, but people won't be searching for that term. Choose a term that will be commonly used and recognized.

Again, Google is the most important. As far as other free resources, I recommend creating lists for Apple Maps, Bing, Yahoo!, Local, Four Square, and Better Business Bureau.

One super important thing to note is your address. Businesses that have a physical presence, commonly called in the business world a "brick and mortar," have a business address they are proud to use. Alternatively, home-based businesses usually do not want to give out their address.

However, don't fall into the trap of just omitting your address altogether. Businesses need to show up on local search engine results even if they don't want customers coming to their location. In this case, I would recommend listing your home address but marking the option on the listing that you don't allow customers at your location. You also could find a friend that is a business owner who will let you take up a "Suite B" mailing address at their location. Another option is getting a PO Box. Not all business directories/search engine results will support a PO Box, but it's better than leaving it blank.

The powerful business listing directories that I haven't mentioned yet are some of the social media platforms, such as Facebook, Instagram, and LinkedIn. This isn't because they are bad, but rather because I'm going a lot further into those in the next chapter. But, they are a powerful way to attract and retain new clients, and they're usually free.

One final note: There are marketing agencies and services that will list your information and distribute it to all of the top directories. As always, you need to ask yourself if it's worth the financial investment.

Chapter 7
Social Media

Social media is a powerful tool for businesses to get their messages out to the masses at, potentially, no cost. I say "potentially" because ads are a common way to increase the results on social media, and they're not free.

Setting up business profiles, inviting friends to follow you, and making posts are free. When you set up a social media account, you need to go ahead and opt to set up a business account, not just a personal account with your business name. Besides following the rules, it allows you to advertise your business and view the analytics on its performance. Several of the platforms require you to first join as a personal user before you can establish a business account.

As far as which social media platforms your business should be on, that can differ from business to business. However, some are the major players that every business can use.

If you'll think back to Chapter 5: Branding, where we defined your ideal target audience, you'll need to have that in mind. Think about the gender and age demographic that represents your most common customer. Ask yourself what social media channels they spend the most time on. Or, better yet, poll some people you know that fit that demographic and ask them which social media channels are their favorites. Find the trends and be on those channels. A business targeting the 60+ demographic probably doesn't belong on TikTok, and a business looking for teens doesn't belong on LinkedIn.

Let's talk through the pros and cons of each of the main channels and which audience it best fits.

Facebook

In the world of social media, Facebook is still king. It is true that a good number of young adults feel Facebook is for "old people," but it is the most commonly used platform for posting pictures and/or text updates.

All businesses should set up a Facebook account because of its value as a business directory and its ability to reach the masses. Facebook is also the best social media channel if you're looking to reach the 55+ crowd. So if you're trying to reach as many people as possible or specifically that senior demographic, Facebook is the way to go.

To set up a business account on Facebook, you have to have a personal account first. There is no password to share with others to let them help manage the Facebook page. Rather, they have to have their own personal profile, and you can grant them admin permission to make changes. We'll call this "Admin Style."

One thing to know about Facebook is the average shelf life of a post is usually three days. If you post something today, your followers could possibly not see it for a couple of days. If you have an event that you are posting about, make sure to do it in advance so everyone sees it before it's too late.

Instagram

Instagram is owned by Meta, which also owns Facebook. Instagram swings a little younger than Facebook does. If you've never used Instagram before, it is similar to Facebook, except it absolutely requires a picture or video for every post. Text is optional. It's more of a viewing experience.

Unlike Facebook where you have to sign up with a personal account, Admin Style, you can establish a password that can be shared with other users. We'll call this "Password Style."

The great thing about Meta owning both Facebook and Instagram is that you can connect these accounts and post to both with a single click. To do that, you have to have them both set up as business accounts, link them together through the settings, and then have a photo on the post (the requirement by Instagram). Once these conditions are met, you can post on both platforms at the same time without having to log in to each. It's a twofer!

LinkedIn

In my opinion, LinkedIn is best for business-to-business businesses, also known as B2B. LinkedIn is a great solution for reaching businesses or professionals.

For example, my marketing agency only sells to businesses. So it's a great fit for me. I've had customers that were executive head hunters (high-end staffing agencies) also do exceptionally well on LinkedIn. If you're needing to hire or market to business professionals, LinkedIn is a great choice.

Like Facebook, LinkedIn is Admin Style where you have to first be a member and then can create a business page. You may decide not to have a business page on LinkedIn, but I think that having a personal profile is a smart move for all business owners. I try to go and connect with people on LinkedIn when I meet them in person.

If you've never used LinkedIn before, it's different from Facebook because it's professionally centered. That makes it far less personal than other social media platforms. I would rarely share a photo of my kids playing sports on LinkedIn unless it was for a business purpose, such as my business sponsored their team and my logo was on the jersey. I might also post the sports photo to show that I finally have achieved a work-life balance so I can make the games. In those cases, my kids' sports pics would be appropriate for LinkedIn.

Twitter

Twitter has a different vibe than the social media platforms mentioned above. For starters, the character limit alone is a differentiator. Twitter limits all posts, called Tweets, to 280 characters. Unlike Facebook where some tend to write a novel for a post, a Tweet is more akin to a sentence or two, short and to the point.

Facebook is more aligned with the people you want to hear from, no matter the topic. Twitter is more aligned around topics you like to read about, no matter who posted it.

The demographic of Twitter is also dispersed. I've seen it used especially well in sharing news headlines with a link. People get sports updates from Twitter, and businesses put out information about outages and special events.

If you want to see a brand having a lot of fun on Twitter, check out @Wendys. Apparently, Wendy grew up to be a smart aleck. It's a prime example of a business embracing its tone of voice and sticking with it so that the personality is memorable.

The shelf life of a Tweet is far shorter than most other social media channels, so you can post to this one more often than the others if that's part of your strategy.

Pinterest

When you think Pinterest, you probably think of recipes, hairstyles, and kitchen remodeling tips. And it definitely is all of those things, but as with all marketing opportunities, you need to remember who your ideal customer is.

If those are the people, namely women, who are going to be reading food and lifestyle articles, then it's a great place for your business to be featured. You'll need to frame your business in a way that will appeal to people looking for that kind of content:

- A cabinet company could showcase pictures of their work and include color and style choices to get that look.
- A lawn company could give tips on the best time of year to plant certain flowers and how to arrange them.

A business account on Pinterest is a Password Style. For the content to be good, it will likely take thought and effort if you're looking for your 'pins' to gain traction for free.

YouTube

YouTube actually has the largest presence online of all the social channels. It has 1.7 billion unique monthly viewers. The trick is it requires video content that people want to watch.

To successfully use YouTube to market your business, you'll need to figure out how to make videos about your brand that people will want to watch. I've seen a dentist make dental videos testing out toothbrushes. There are chiropractors popping all sorts of joints. Speaking of popping, dermatologists make those videos too.

What do you do that someone would want to watch? If you can answer that question, and actually do it consistently, then YouTube is a powerful marketing tool to tap into.

Additionally, YouTube is owned by Google, and Google seems to like people playing nicely with their entities, so it can be useful in the long run for SEO strategy.

This is also a Password Style, and it's no coincidence that the same account you need for your Google business directory will work for YouTube.

TikTok

If you want to reach the younger demographic, TikTok is a great way to do it. The biggest age demographic for TikTok users is 16-24.

TikTok lets you post 15- to 60-second videos. To successfully capture attention on this platform, you probably will need to be flashy and trendy. It's not the platform for typical business ads.

Reaching ages 16-24 would be great for colleges, tutoring services, car dealerships, clothing brands, and pretty much any products and services aimed at young adults. A TikTok account is Password Style.

Snapchat

Snapchat is another way to target a younger audience with 70 percent of users under the age of 34. I find it a little harder to use in business because it's mobile-only, and a lot of the business scheduling tools don't play friendly with it.

Utilizing the tool to show behind-the-scenes looks at your business or someone really enjoying your product or service could be great for branding. There are also interesting advertising options on this channel. It is a Password Style account.

More good things to know

I just mentioned using a social media scheduling tool for social media. When managing their personal accounts, most people make social media posts when the mood strikes. But, for a lot of people, the mood doesn't strike nearly often enough to actually count as marketing.

And you don't want to be tied to your computer for posting especially on weekends and holidays. There are free tools available that allow you to schedule your posts to go out on multiple platforms when you want them to post. These tools make the task of posting less overwhelming than posting on your own, and they can guarantee that your posts go out on a regular basis. We typically post a month at a time for most of our social media customers and modify/add as exceptions or new opportunities arise. Google "free social media scheduling tool" and decide which option best suits your needs.

Because we're wanting the SEO benefit, make sure to set up the profiles completely on your social media, using the exact name, address, and phone numbers. Take the time to list all of your products and services and pertinent details.

To get the most out of your social media channels, one thing important is to keep it social. People don't sign in hoping for the chance to watch advertising pitches. They want to be entertained, informed, or intrigued. Keep your posts social. Use your tone of voice established in your branding.

Users especially like seeing people, animals, and movement in posts. If you want to slow the scroll, try to add graphics/images that catch the user's attention. Ask questions. When people comment and engage, it actually tells the "algorithms" that people like the post, and it will likely be shown to more users. When you have a good post, ask people to share it and give them a reason. For example, "Please help share this post to let as many people as possible know about our local business."

While we're on the topic of keeping social media social, by all means, reply to comments! It shows that you are engaged and encourages more conversation.

The big rule is to post regularly. You don't want users to scroll your channel and wonder if you're out of business because you haven't posted recently. Choose the social media channels that you can reasonably maintain well and post regularly. A good rule of thumb is to post at least once a week.

Take advantage of ways you can work smarter. For example, use social media scheduling tools that let you post once for multiple channels. Try different tricks, like linking Facebook and Instagram. Above all, just post.

All of the social media channels I've mentioned offer paid advertising options. Buying ads on social media can help your business. But this is a book about building your *Shoestring Empire* and posting about your business is a free way to build buzz and generate leads.

Chapter 8
Next Steps

Now that your digital presence is established, let's talk about getting your business up and running. Some may think I've put the cart before the horse, but I believe that getting your online synergies established as soon as possible and getting excitement and demand before you launch is key. You can use this online presence to recruit employees as well. It is, of course, your decision. If I knew your particulars, I might even agree to reverse the order, but as I rule, this is the order that I recommend.

What comes next depends upon you and your business. If it's a service business, you may be ready to start servicing customers. But you still have questions:

- What do you need to start your business?
- A brick-and-mortar location?
- A website?
- Products?

You definitely need to figure this out. Let's explore some possibilities. We'll start with service businesses and then move on to product businesses.

Service businesses

In my opinion, service businesses are cheaper to start but harder to scale. For example, to start a massage business, all you need is a table, a sheet, and some lotion. That's a low startup cost. It's harder to scale because your time performing this service is your bottleneck. It's hard to provide your quality of service with someone else's hands.

If you truly have a shoestring budget, I want you to seriously consider starting without a brick-and-mortar for your business if it's at all possible. The massage therapist, for example, can be mobile and travel to clients' homes until generating enough business to justify a brick-and-mortar expense.

It would be a shame to spend the entire startup budget on a location and not have the money on hand to get people to it (marketing). Brick-and-mortar locations require more money than it seems. On top of rent, you need furniture, wifi, paper towels, and all sorts of little things that may not be in your plans.

If you do decide that you absolutely need a brick-and-mortar for your service business, I highly recommend checking with your chamber of commerce. I know of several that have business incubators that offer reduced rent in an effort to increase the number of businesses operating in their cities.

Check to see if this type of offer is available. That's how I started my service business.

Are you wondering why I didn't take my own advice and start my business at home? It's a fair question. Starting my marketing agency in my home was a poor choice for me because I get distracted too easily at home. I couldn't stay focused in that setting. Maybe you can, but I needed the brick-and-mortar to make it work for me.

You might need to experiment by spending time with yourself. If you find it difficult to work from home, you might be able to improve your attention span with practice. Or you might decide you need to do what I did, not what I said.

If your business plans never include a brick-and-mortar location, you should plan for a website for your business. With no physical presence to establish credibility, you especially need a virtual presence for that exact same reason.

I'll confess my bias. I build websites for a living, but I really believe that this is the right answer. Either I've drunk the Kool-Aid, or I'm just correct (I think it's both). People want to feel that you are a professional, well-established business. A social media channel is great, but just not the same. People want to:

- see your services listed in one place so they don't have to scroll forever
- see testimonials from your clients
- learn more about you

A website is where you can put all these elements together to showcase your business and ask your reader to choose you.

Product businesses

If you're starting a product business, the first thing to decide is if you are going to stock inventory or buy it or make it on demand.

Stocking inventory is a great decision for items that require a long lead time. For example, a potter would need a minimum of a week to make a piece of pottery once you factor in making it, letting it dry, firing it, glazing it, packing it, and shipping it. Actually, a week is probably unrealistic. If you had several styles that you make, then having a few on hand, selling those, and then replenishing can free up the potter's time to not always be on standby to drop everything whenever an order comes in.

However, this inventory style restricts you from selling custom orders, which can be a part of your business model. It's a matter of balance.

Stocking inventory makes sense, but it's costly. To start with, you need a place to store your goods before you sell them. In addition, inventory can degrade, walk away, or become obsolete. It also ties up your resources until you can sell them.

I don't have an answer or even a recommendation. You need to think through your business model and decide what makes the most sense to you.

The next major decision is where you are going to sell your products:

- in person?
- online?

If your answer is in person, you'll need to decide where. The cheaper option would be a pop-up presence. I know businesses that started with booths at flea markets, live events, and seasonal markets. These are great ways to sell products in person without much overhead.

As with the service business, I'd also recommend checking with a business incubator for a low-rent storefront. A food truck type of setup could be another way to get your business going. I'm not calling a food truck cheap, just less than most brick-and-mortar locations.

The important thing to remember, whether your business is in a storefront or online, you have to tell people about it — also known as "marketing" — to get people to patronize it. There are possible exceptions. For example, if your storefront is in the middle of a busy mall selling something desired by the masses, your location could be enough. But for most businesses, don't bank on your online or physical presence alone to attract customers. Instead of "If you build it, they will come," I say, "If you market it, they will come."

Chapter 9
Legal Advice

If you are ready to form your business, you have to make it legal. In my few years as a business owner, I have needed more legal counsel than I have required in the rest of my life combined.

It starts early with articles of incorporation. The needs multiply when you take on investors, employees, or even clients. You'll likely want someone to glance at your sales contracts if possible to see if they are actionable. If you have legal action taken against you or receive imposing letters in the mail that frighten you, it is good to know up front where you can find help without breaking the bank.

If you have questions about the rules and regulations of government agencies, like the IRS, FTC, ADA, or OSHA, you can reach out to them directly. It is in their own interest to help you comply.

These agencies are looking out for their own interests, so they will definitely have accurate information. However, they may or may not take the time to discuss how the law applies to your personal situation. In my experience, it's often the luck of the draw in who you reach when you contact them for how extra-mile helpful they will be.

Next, consider pro bono (Latin for "free") workshops on important topics. There are sometimes free legal opportunities in areas such as clinics run by law students working to earn experience. If you're lucky, you may have a friend who's a lawyer and will point you in the right direction.

It's possible you could trade services with them. If you're a hairdresser, you could have a monthly appointment in which you do your magic on her (or his wife), and during that time, you can bounce ideas off of your legal counsel. (For my lawyer friend, thank you!)

If you can get free advice, that's a great way to get going. But as with any relationship, if it's always one-sided or thankless, the well dries up eventually. Recognize what you are offering in trade and act accordingly.

Even though I have a fabulous lawyer friend who has given me counsel on all of my major needs, there is no way I would bombard her with every little thing. I'm able to handle 99 percent of my questions without her even knowing about them, which may be why she's always so willing to answer when I bring my one-percent questions to her.

Since I'm not a lawyer, I take advantage of online legal tools to draft all of my:

- contracts
- non-competes

- NDAs (non-disclosure agreements)
- employment contracts
- terminations
- and more

Here are resources that may help you.

Google

It might seem silly to add Google to the list, but that's the first place I go when I have a question. There are multiple warnings I would add before you let any random stranger on the world wide web chart your legal fate by what they have written:

- First, make sure the source you are using is credible. When I have a question on employment security, I want the source to be an authority on state and federal regulations.
- Second, this is a great way to find information on little questions, but not on the big stuff. You'll need a professional for that.
- Third, it needs to make sense to you. Don't just copy and paste legal jargon that you don't understand into your documents. The legal jargon is used to make contracts airtight, but if you don't know what you're saying and it isn't coming from a professional representing you, it

may mean something vastly different than you intended.

With those three caveats in mind, you can search online for some great resources for your specific legal questions. And it's a free solution.

Online software

There are multiple websites online that help you draft airtight legal documents that just allow you to answer some questions to fill in the details. This is the online tool that I mentioned earlier where I handle the vast majority of my legal needs without consulting a professional. There are usually fees for using the service, but it's much less than a single hour of consultation with a professional attorney.

Your options include:

• avvo.com: It lists thousands of attorneys with their specialties, ratings, and reviews. If you are looking to hire an attorney and have no idea where to start, this may be a good place. In addition, approximately 20,000 legal questions have been asked at the time of this writing, and most have been answered by multiple attorneys with sound advice. Some of those answers point toward consulting with an attorney, but that is probably the way that situation needed to be handled. If you have time to wait for a response, it could be a free way to get your question answered.

- freeadvice.com: This service centers on the idea of scheduling a free consultation with a lawyer within your needed area of expertise. It has a robust question-and-answer section. I have no doubt the free consultation service is a wonderful resource, but I'd advise you to prepare to say, "No," to their paid counsel unless it's in your best interest. Their free consultation may be a goodwill gesture, but it's also a sales tool. Paid legal advice is a wonderful thing that could make or break your business, but it shouldn't be something you back into because you made an impulsive decision or weren't prepared to say, "No."

- lawyers.com and lawguru.com: These websites offer a wealth of information on various legal topics. You can browse by interest, or you can search for your specific question. I can get lost in the search topics because I tend to hoard information. If you have a question, you can find where someone else has already asked it. You also can ask your own question. I prefer the instant gratification of finding it already answered, but you do have to make sure the circumstances are relevant to your situation. The main goal of the sites seems to be referring you to a paid attorney, but you can take advantage of the Q&A for free.

- legalzoom.com: You select the service you need, and there is a flat-rate fee to get the job done. It isn't instant. There are lists of how long it will take to get certain legal documents written up and filed on your behalf. You can pay extra in some cases to get it done faster. It handles common services around business formation, including forming your LLC, corporation or non-profit. The site handles wills and trusts as well as intellectual property issues about copyrights and patents. The prices are surprisingly affordable in my opinion, but I am a cheapskate at heart. This might be a great way to pay a one-time fee to get a service done and not have to worry about hourly charges or forgetting to turn off a subscription.

- rocketlawyer.com: This service allows you to create online legal documents by answering questions, and it adds all the legalese to make it effective. They also send out the documents to the recipients for signature and keep a record of your contracts. With this service, you can pay per document or sign up for a monthly subscription. If you use the service fairly regularly, it would definitely be more cost-effective to subscribe. In addition, you can ask questions of on-call lawyers and get 30 minutes of support for new questions. This is included with the subscription and at a flat rate for non-subscribers. If you want to do this on a budget, take advantage of a free seven-day trial, get as many legal documents created as you can in that timeframe, and then cancel. The paid subscription will be worthwhile for many business owners.

I'm sure my brilliant lawyer friend would advise me at this point to remind you that I am not a trained attorney and nothing I have written should be taken as legal advice but is only my observations as a business owner.

Chapter 10

Mental Readiness

I'm not a regular exerciser. I go for a while and quit. Eventually, I start over with the same result. I'm not proud of it. It's just a fact. I find myself fighting against my mind. I decide:

- Something is too hard without trying it.
- I'm too tired before I get up.
- I'll do it later, which doesn't happen often.

I'm not fighting against sore muscles or fatigue but my own brain.

There will be a point when starting your business gets hard. Filing your LLC is exhilarating and takes just a few minutes. Making a list of the products or services you're selling is great. Touring office locations puts you on Cloud Nine.

For all the fun activities, there probably will be things that trip you up. It could be a lack of money to pay for the things you want. It could be talking to a discouraging person. It could be legitimate fatigue from pulling double time in your present job and new business. There's almost always something hidden in the weeds and waiting for the opportunity to jump out and steal your motivation. You need to plan ahead for this eventuality, so you have the resources ready when this particular monster attacks.

I work through issues that seem overwhelming by thinking of worst-case scenarios. That may seem pessimistic, but I like knowing the worst that can happen and deciding what to do before it happens. Once I come to terms with the worst-case possibility, I know I can handle anything else.

One worst-case scenario I worked through when starting my business was not being able to get new customers. If that happened, I could cut my losses, find a job for my employee, sell off the equipment/furniture, and find a new job for myself. I'd have to work for a while to pay off my debts, but I could do it. For me, it would be less money lost than buying a car. It would stink. It'd bruise my ego, but I could live with it.

As most often happens with worst-case scenarios we dream up, that one never materialized. However, by thinking about the real possibility, I was able to go forward with a plan.

Whenever problems arise, there are almost always options. If you can't figure out a problem, check with your mentor. If money is the issue, go to your representative from the Small Business Association. Talk to your local community bank. Talk to your credit union. If you're stuck, find someone to help you get unstuck.

If taking out a loan is not in your cards, consider taking on a partner. If I'm being honest, I don't see 50/50 partnerships ending well. Even the 50/50 partnership we call marriage has an average lifespan of only 8.2 years. But you can take on a minority or silent partner. They can contribute financially, own a piece of the business, and get periodic updates on the state of affairs. You will have to work out the terms, but it's a viable option if traditional financing doesn't work for you.

If you're considering taking on a business partner, I suggest making your intentions known in the business community. I had several offers to invest in my business when I started out, and I have met multiple business investors along the way. From a business investor's standpoint, all they have to do is let you borrow some money and then get payouts and ownership.

Since we're talking about money, one of my favorite local business owners recently reminded me that you don't need a year's worth of rent and salary to get going. All you need is enough for one month. After that, you can figure it out again the next month.

And the next.

And the next.

If that doesn't line up with your comfort level, you can figure out a different plan. But he's right. You just need your mind ready to own that risk.

As far as naysayers, they will always exist. I've learned that people with negative things to say usually have their own issues that have nothing to do with you or your business.

Bullies prey on the weak as a reflection of how they feel about themselves. Those showing you the most grief are likely frustrated with themselves for not having the courage to pursue something so daring.

You can prepare yourself by actually rehearsing what you'd say to someone trying to discourage you. If you quit because of their words, you just let them control the direction of your life. Keep your power and use it to overcome more worthy opponents than those that come bearing gifts of fear and doubt.

There is a point in time in every big project when the newness and excitement wear off. Whenever I have to move from one house to another, it's exciting at first to start packing my favorite treasures. It's also satisfying to move the big pieces of furniture. You can see momentous progress as each piece vacates its previous home.

Then you're left with the drawers. It's always the drawers. You feel practically finished, but your energy wanes, and it takes an hour to go through a single drawer. That's the point where you want to just dump all the contents in a pile and strike a match.

You may reach a point in your business where you feel like that. In that case, you need to remind yourself why you started in the first place. Why were you excited? Rekindle your spark, so it can keep firing your progress.

A couple of years ago, I adopted this quote as my motto: "I fear regret more than I fear failure."

I looked it up and found it attributed to multiple authors, so I don't know who said it first. I do know what it means to me. It has done wonders for my mental game. I cannot imagine being 100 years old and regretting that I tried. What's worse than failing is never trying and having to live with that cowardice your entire life. While writing *Shoestring Empire*, my first business is only a few years old. There may come a day when I have to hang my head in defeat. But the joy of business ownership is something no one can ever take away from me.

As Erin Hanson said, "What if I fall? But oh, my darling. What if you fly?"

Go! Go! Go!

Go! Go! Go!

Chapter 11
Borrowing Credibility

When I was growing up, my mom always gave my dad his haircuts. I'm not talking about buzzing it off with clippers. I'm talking about the super shiny metal scissors and a comb. It takes skill and precision. I watched her do this monthly for my entire upbringing. I always asked if I could be the one to do it.

Here's a simple fact: Haircuts are unforgiving. There is no un-cutting. Sure, it will grow back, but he'd have to display my handiwork for weeks. In college, my at-the-time boyfriend always got professional haircuts, and he wasn't willing to consider turning his hair into my DIY project. I had to live with knowing in my gut that I could do it, but no volunteers were willing to let me prove it.

One day, my family was planning to go to a fancy celebratory meal. My dad needed a haircut. My mom's work had run long, so she was unavailable to administer it.

My dad told me, "This is your big break, kid!"

I ran excitedly to get the scissors and comb. My dad thought I had too much enthusiasm, but I gave him his haircut, and he was pleased. I was a haircutter. My then-boyfriend was there and saw my handiwork. Since my dad looked good, he gave me a chance to cut his hair as well, and I have been his barber for the past 20 years.

It was frustrating to know I could do something but couldn't get the chance to prove it. I was lacking credibility as a barber. If I'm completely honest, I probably wouldn't have given myself a chance either. To get started in any new skill worth doing, you need to establish credibility for yourself.

Haircutting is not my vocation or even a side hustle. I'm a marketer, but breaking into marketing was no less challenging. Someone had to take a chance on me and my skills. I needed that first person to put their faith in me. I somehow convinced a well-respected retail establishment to trust me. I underpriced my services by at least one decimal point, which may be why they accepted my offer in the first place. What I did next was the key. I gave them something well beyond their expectations. They were proud to show it off, and so was I.

After that website went live, I used it as an example to show my abilities to other businesses that I hoped to work with. When they saw it, they didn't know my name, but they knew the name of that business, so I essentially borrowed their credibility. Once I had done what I do a thousand times over (I could be exaggerating), I didn't need their credibility because I had my own. Getting started was the tricky part.

Borrowing Credibility

How can you borrow credibility? A lot of businesses can follow my model exactly. A photographer can take some incredible shots of their chosen subject for free or cheap and build a portfolio. When your target is residential clients, you could do the same thing, choosing a prominent community member and using their name for your credibility. You can take before and after pictures or get a testimonial, with their permission, to share with potential new customers.

If you legitimately have credibility, you need to showcase that to make it seem like choosing you is less risky. If you don't already have an established name for yourself in your market and industry, connect the dots for your potential customers and make it easy for them to lend you trust.

Do you have XX years of experience in XX city? Showcase that.

Do you have degrees, training certifications, awards, commendations, etc? Let your customers know about it.

As business owners, we all know we need to market our businesses, but we somehow seem to forget we need to market ourselves as well.

Nobody wants to receive your first haircut. No one pays a premium for your first wedding cake. In that situation, they are taking a risk on you. Do what you can to assume that risk yourself by going above and beyond to either make it worthwhile to your customer or give them some kind of guarantee that makes it easier.

A "money-back guarantee" is a popular way of assuming the risk for your customer. Figure out what makes sense in your profession, and make it easier for your new clients to say, "Yes," to you while you're getting established.

Chapter 12
Smarter and Harder

I once had a mentor who was a super-successful salesperson. He wasn't flashy, but that was a choice. He was his organization's top seller year after year. I wanted to know how he did it.

Did his daddy have golfing buddies who owed him favors? Good guess, but that's not it.

Did he have a single customer that got incredibly huge and pulled all of his numbers up? That's not it either.

One day, I asked for his secret, and he told me.

"Some people think you should work smarter, not harder. And that's good advice, but it hasn't gotten me to where I am today. Do you really want to know how I did it?" he said.

I nodded my head vigorously. I didn't want to speak for fear of making him change his mind.

He smiled, leaned in, looked me in the eye, and said, "I cheat!"

What?! Your big answer is you cheat?! Surely this was a joke.

After giving me a minute to let my brain unravel, he told me calmly:

"You see, my work schedule is Monday to Friday from 8 to 5. That's fine, but if I want to get in with the plant managers from 8 to 5, I have to go in the proper door, get the proper passes, check in with the correct receptionist, and follow the procedure.

"That procedure is designed to keep people like me out. So instead of doing that for months on end hoping my persistence finally pays off and they grant me a meeting, I simply asked his receptionist about what time the plant manager comes into work each day. She didn't know but told me early, before she got there each day.

"The next morning, I arrived at 6 am with a box of donuts and a large coffee, parked next to the plant manager's parking spot, and waited. When he pulled in, I was waiting on him with a big, genuine smile, a box of donuts, and an outstretched hand.

"He was shocked to see me there at that hour but it told him I was willing to do whatever needed to be done to service his account. He appreciated my gumption, and I got the business.

"In fact, I got a lot of businesses to sign on in that manner. Not all 6 a.m. donut calls, but thinking outside the box to push through the red tape."

That moment was life-changing for me. I'm very much a play-by-the-rules kind of gal. But I can be creative. I can think outside the box to find new solutions to old problems. And I'm definitely not afraid to work hard. My mentor doesn't work smarter or harder. He works smarter AND harder!

So, how can we work smarter and harder? I think one way we can do that is by standing on the shoulders of giants. Find someone else who is doing well and use them as a template. Build your business from there.

I don't have to invent what a great website looks or acts like. I need to find some truly great websites, use them as my baseline, and then find ways to make mine even better. This concept applies to every business. That's the work smarter part.

As for working harder, you want to think about the time you put in each day and how you use it. Of course, you want to serve your customers because that's how you get paid. You also want to spend time learning and practicing to get better because that's how you'll get paid more in the future.

Another way that I work smarter is by hiring talented people. For example, I have a business coach who has helped many others grow their businesses. I'm leveraging her knowledge and best practices to grow my business.

I have super-talented designers and programmers who do the heavy lifting on major projects. They're under my direction but working in tandem to tap into their individual strengths and build upon the strengths of others.

You may not start out with a team, especially if you're on a shoestring budget. For the record, I had a team of one when I first started. If you're able to start with helpers, use them to work smarter and harder. Consider recruiting employees that have different strengths than you, so you have multiple ways to serve your customers' needs.

Another way to get the most out of everything you do is to use readily available resources. I have exceptional programmers and designers on my team. I could easily have them craft a proprietary system to send newsletters to customers. But with Mail Chimp and Constant Contact being so affordable and possibly free, why would I do that? By using those services, I can have my team focused on what they do best.

This example is specific to my field but relevant to every single one:

- Why should a doctor spend his hours documenting accounting transactions when he can use software like Quickbooks?
- Why should an animator draw out every single frame when she could draw the major details and use software to fill in the in-between parts?

Find shortcuts in your business that don't sacrifice quality, and use them so your time can be invested in more important areas.

In my business, I cheat just like my mentor told me to do, and you can too. Look for unique opportunities. Look at your competitors and see what they are doing well. Notice what they're doing poorly as well, so you can do it better and position your business as an expert on that exact thing.

Consider reaching out to businesses similar to yours in different markets and ask for a few minutes of their time. Not only do people love talking about themselves, but there's a good chance someone once helped them along the way, so you're giving them an opportunity to pay it forward.

Work smarter.

Work harder.

When you get tired, rest and then start over. It will pay off one day, and you can prop your feet up on your desk in your office with a view and reflect on how all of your hard work paid off.

Chapter 13

When to Spend

This book is based on starting your business with a shoestring budget, but it's not about building a zero-cost business.

And starting with a small budget does not mean you'll always have a small budget. In fact, we hope just the opposite. There are times when not spending money is a poor decision.

This book is not a land-of-a scarcity-mentality. It's just the opposite. It's about finding ways to say, "Yes," even when your bank account might look like a, "No!" There is no business in existence that somebody didn't spend some money on, so let's examine ways to spend *well*.

We've already talked about whether or not a business should initially invest in a brick-and-mortar building. Here's a quick refresher:

- If it makes sense, do it.
- If it doesn't, don't.

Now, let's dig into some other issues.

Should I buy equipment?

Equipment, especially equipment pertinent to what you do, is important. In the long run, owning is much cheaper than renting. The question to consider is, if you buy, will you have money left to operate and market your business? A lot of people think of marketing as a luxury in business, but often it determines if your phone rings or not.

If your business legitimately needs a piece of equipment, think about how often your business will use it. If it's seldom, once a month or less, renting might free up space in your budget for other priorities. If it's daily, it's something worth serious consideration. You don't need a tractor to sell your land-clearing services. You need a picture of a tractor on your website or marketing materials, and you need to know where to get one when you need it.

If you don't have the credit or capital to purchase, leasing may be your only option, and that's OK. I don't know your specifics, but a great accountant could be your new best friend. If it'd cost more to rent at the frequency you need it and your need is a long-term need, try to find a way to save money by purchasing.

Should I hire an employee?

I have employees. I LOVE my employees. But it's no secret that employees are expensive. Not only do they want a paycheck every week, but they also need things like computers, toilet paper, chairs, etc. And whatever you agree to pay them per hour, it costs way more than that. You have to pay taxes and insurance, and that's not even considering benefits.

But do you know what's even more expensive than employees? Losing work because you don't have enough time to fulfill the orders, or even worse, having a poor reputation for shoddy work because you didn't have enough time to do the job well. When you are so constrained that you have no time to quote new jobs or network and make new connections, you need help. But that does not mean you need to rush to hire a full-time employee.

Let's first talk about contractors. When you have an employee, you have to pay taxes and unemployment benefits and assume liability for their wellbeing. A contractor, on the other hand, is self-employed, and you are essentially their customer. Although you need to be a good person and honor your commitments, a contractor is a much lower responsibility on the workforce scale.

You'll need to check your state's rules about contractors to make sure you're in compliance. In my state, it's fairly lax. In many businesses, a sales force works for commission only, so if they make no sales, they make no money. The downside to hiring contractors is that, when the economy is employee-driven, many people have options and may find a more attractive offer elsewhere. Additionally, if you are seeking skilled or top talent, you may not have a long-term employee with a contract-only offer.

Next, consider using services from other vendors instead of hiring your own. I don't hire an accountant. I only use the services of one. I don't employ handymen, pest control agents, or lawn care men, but businesses have these services for hire.

Another venue that I've only recently discovered is the blossoming field of virtual assistants. You can log online, choose a skillset that you need help with, interview people with experience in your need, assign tasks, get your work done, and repeat. If you don't like your VA, ask for a reassignment. If you don't see the value, terminate the contract. No layoffs. No hurt feelings. The downside is VAs run somewhere around $30 per hour. That may sound high when compared with high school or college-aged helpers, but if they can save your sanity and keep you from needing to hire additional employees, it could provide cost savings.

My word of caution around hiring other businesses to help with your business through contract services is this: **Never outsource your core competencies.**

The thing that makes your business special shouldn't be outsourced. Not only are you not providing your customers the things you are best at, but you're also at the mercy of another business to fulfill the things to make you look good. If they fail, you fail.

In my business, design is one of our core competencies. We do all of our design work in-house, and that won't change. But actually scheduling social media posts on the various social media platforms isn't something that people will notice or care about if we don't do it ourselves. We just have to ensure it's done well. You may want to take time to sketch out a list of your tasks and highlight or asterisk the ones that are your core competencies, those products or services that will make or break your business. Make sure they stay under your control.

Next, even if you choose to hire an employee, you may be able to only use part-time help instead of a full-time employee. There are many people out there who don't need or want full-time employment, and they're willing to alleviate your needs without a 40-hour-a-week commitment. Consider retirees, stay-at-home moms that want a little something to do while their kids are in school, people looking for a second job for extra income, and students. Those are all great candidates for people that may prefer part-time hours. There is nothing more frustrating for a small business owner than to have an underutilized employee who gets full-time pay. You can always add more help down the road if you realize the part-time status is insufficient. In my state, 32 hours per week is the magical cutoff number between part-time and full-time, but you'll need to check your local rules to be sure.

There is a chance that you may benefit from hiring a full-time employee. I've seen businesses fail to launch because the owner tried to do it all by himself, wore himself out, disappointed his customers, and lacked the time to go out and make new customers. I've seen businesses peak at the capacity of the owner and plateau. An employee is not necessarily a bad thing, I just wanted you to consider the alternatives, so you can make an informed decision when hiring full-time employees.

Should I decorate my business?

Many business owners pay to decorate their offices before the grand opening. This can be paintings for the wall, pillows to go on the sofas, and other pleasant touches.

If the expenditure is not actually a decoration but rather a demarcation, as in signage to let customers know you are there and in business, it is probably a good idea within reason. With a shoestring budget, I wouldn't start out with a 20-foot LED sign, but you do want people to notice your business.

I'll also say that cleanliness is not optional for the physical appearance of your business. A gallon of paint and elbow grease can accomplish great things.

If your business is super high-end with luxury prices, you need the details to make people feel you are worth the expense. If not, making your business feel pulled together is wonderful, but it shouldn't be done at the expense of other necessary operating expenses.

Before you invest a lot of money into your physical office, ask yourself how much of your business transactions will happen in-office. If you are a therapist, it may be almost all of them. As a marketing agency, shockingly few of my clients come to the office. I bought all of the rugs and plants and could have probably skimped a little at first. Hindsight is 2020, right?

Should I market my business?

Finally, you should know by now how I feel about marketing. I am, after all, a marketer by trade. But is it a worthwhile investment when money is tight?

I've heard business after business say they will invest in marketing when the business picks up. If you legitimately do not have the money to invest in marketing, utilizing credit is a hard decision that would give me pause as well. But marketing can make the phone ring. A good rule of thumb is 2-5% of revenue for a B2B business and 5-10% for B2C companies.

If you really can't afford marketing, invest extra care in networking, word-of-mouth marketing, and social media marketing until you're able to increase your marketing budget.

Here's the exception: If you have so much business you can't take in more clients, you're among the lucky few that get to relax on this. But remember, other businesses are actively working to take your customers.

Always be marketing.

Chapter 14

Lean, not Cheap

I've spent a whole book telling you when not to spend, and in my opinion, it's all good advice, but I do want to note that cheap isn't always the best. The purpose of this book is to show you how to start a business without an abundance of resources. I want to help eliminate the fear that comes from the financial responsibilities of a business.

But I would be remiss if I left you with the impression that it's always best to save money. There are things you can do yourself that you also could pay someone else to do. There also are things that you can't do yourself even if you invest the time. Some products and services are worth paying for.

One thing that seems easy to save money on is taxes. Hiring a CPA can easily cost $500+, especially when they begin filing for both your business and personal taxes. With so many online tools, it is quite easy to file your own taxes online or to use a cheaper walk-in type of service to file your taxes. I'm sure they all do a good job and check the correct boxes. I have talked to many business owners who have saved money by filing their own taxes.

However, the advice that top-notch tax advisors offer is sometimes priceless or, at least, worth many times more than their fees. A good CPA will not only file your taxes on time but will advise you during the tax year, so you can take advantage of the rules and regulations:

- If you're having a profitable year, a CPA may advise you to invest in your business to avoid a hefty tax bill.
- A knowledgeable advisor can help you take advantage of credits and minimize tax obligations.
- If things go crazy, they could even keep you out of jail by preventing faulty financial decisions.

If you happen to be a highly experienced tax expert, I'm sure you could handle this on your own, but for the rest of us, it's worth the price to hire a professional.

Another thing that you could but shouldn't save money on is outsourcing what you're best at. Ask yourself the question, "What problem is my business solving?" The answer may surprise you.

For example, I know from experience that many marketing agencies outsource the creation of their work. They have local sellers who talk to the client, but the actual work is done in a different state or country. If that business feels that the problem they are solving is consulting with local businesses and giving advice, then it doesn't matter that their work is outsourced. If, however, it's the actual product quality that is the solution they are providing, then outsourcing the work is giving away control over the quality. It's possible to control the quality but not the production, but it requires serious managerial skills. Take a moment to become crystal clear on what your business's purpose is.

Once again: **Never outsource your core competency**.

Another no-no in going cheap is filling your plate so full that you can't spend time on your business. As a business owner, I do it myself. If I need a task done and there is no one with the time or skills to do it, I often put it on my own to-do list whether or not it is my strength.

I do all of the payroll at my business. I don't have a calling to do payroll nor did I have prior experience executing the task, but there was no one else to do it, so it went on my list. Who orders the coffee and trash bags? That went on my list too. These two tasks are small, but when you keep stacking and stacking, they add up. If I'm not careful, I can fill my 40+ hours each week working in my business and forsake working on my business.

Working on my business is a far different task that involves

- having meetings with employees
- giving feedback
- evaluating profits and losses

- making decisions
- hiring and firing
- dealing with legal issues
- deciding on promotions
- looking for new opportunities

I am the only person that can make strategic decisions for my business. If I allow myself to become so bogged down with those add-on tasks, it is easy for the things I need to do to go undone. I can have the illusion of productivity without delivering critical results. If this is you, you need to invest in some help so that you can do the things that only you can do. Let someone else take the generic tasks off your plate.

This lean-not-cheap attitude also applies to insuring your business. I'm the type of gal who usually doesn't pay for extended warranties. I don't buy protection plans. I don't upgrade to get my plane tickets reimbursable. I save money on lots of little instances like that. With each of those decisions, I ask myself if I can afford to lose my investment in them, and if I can afford it, I'm usually willing to take the risk of having to do just that. Usually, I don't have to pay to replace it. I'm essentially self-insuring those purchases.

In spite of that, when it comes to general liability insurance on your business, most small businesses can't afford to self-insure against something like a lawsuit. If someone gets injured on your watch or you accidentally do damage to another entity, those types of things can make even stable businesses go belly-up. If you can't afford the loss, you need to insure it.

There are millions of ways to save money in your business, but as the saying goes, it costs money to make money. You will need to spend on some things. Always look for ways to save money but not at the expense of long-term success. Evaluate each expense, do your research, check with mentors, and decide accordingly.

Chapter 15
Free Resources

I know some great strategic planners. They've got the long game figured out. They're working on 10-year plans and chipping away at strategic mini-steps along the way. I wish that starting my business was something I'd been working toward for a decade, but the simple truth is, there was a straw that broke the camel's back, so in less than six weeks, I was sitting in my new office.

Obviously, I pulled a lot of things together very quickly while still giving a full-time effort at my job in the meantime. I have since learned about resources that are available online that I wasn't aware of when I started my business. I wish I would have known about them during those early days. This isn't an exhaustive list. You should do your own research, but I will share with you some free resources worth checking out.

Chamber of Commerce

Ok, I did actually use this resource when starting my business, and it went well. I highly recommend reaching out to your local chamber if you are starting a business. It is literally their mission to encourage, support, and promote businesses in their area. They don't hand out free money, but they do hand out free advice, like the pros and cons of filing an LLC with your secretary of state's office.

I started out in a low-rent business incubator. It was a resource provided by my chamber of commerce. They commonly have ribbon cuttings for new locations, tell you about networking opportunities, and most importantly, mention your name in a room full of opportunities. Chambers also can connect you with information about local grants and tax advantages. However, they can't do any of that if they don't know you and your business.

Chamber representatives likely will ask your business to join and become a member. In my opinion, it is well worth the cost. Membership has served my business well. I urge you to at least check in with your chamber and look for opportunities to collaborate.

Small Business Association (SBA)

The SBA has a wealth of knowledge. There are tools on www.sba.gov that help you plan, launch, manage, and grow your business. They have calculators and tools, webinars, and counseling. Don't let the word "small" fool you here either.

Their definition of the word varies from industry to industry. In general, it means less than 250 employees, and your revenue can sometimes be in the millions before you're no longer considered a small business.

But they're never going to show up at your door telling you they're ready to help. It is your job to reach out, use their tools, register for their webinars, ask for a mentor, and apply for loans. It is an extension of the government designed and funded to assist small businesses that are starting out or scaling up.

If you hire a business coach, they push you and suggest resources and tools. With the SBA, you have to go after what you need. But the resources are free, and many are fantastic.

SCORE

SCORE is provided by the SBA. It exists for the purpose of business mentoring. Officials have assembled a band of volunteer mentors willing to help your business succeed. They also put on high-quality webinars that have been instrumental in my business. In fact, I got the idea for writing this book at a SCORE webinar. I've attended webinars on

- preparing for taxes
- stress management
- public speaking
- many others

They don't hand out money, but they offer information you can use to both save and make money for your business.

Procurement Technical Assistance Center (PTAC)

If you're interested in gaining government contracts for your products or services, PTAC is a government agency that helps small businesses bid on, win, and fulfill government contracts.

The world of government contracting can be scary and overwhelming from an outsider's perspective, so an agency like this can be extremely helpful. While the government is extremely price-sensitive, different agencies have the need to buy large contracts all the time. If your business could benefit from government contracts, this resource is highly recommended.

No one will ever care as much about your business as you do. You cannot place the burden of responsibility for your success on anyone else's shoulders. So use these excellent free services with the upfront understanding that you will have to take the initiative. You will have to do the research. You will have to be your own advocate and, possibly, the squeaky wheel. These are tools you can use to build and scale your business.

Scale It Up

Chapter 16
Marketing

Marketing is how you let people know about your business. It's how you share your business with the world. It's pushing your brand, products, and services out into your community instead of waiting for potential customers to stumble across your business.

In this chapter, we'll discuss:

- various marketing initiatives
- costs involved
- work involved
- tools you can use

Let's dive in.

Maybe it's a pet peeve of mine, but word of mouth is not a marketing strategy. Let's clear that up right away. Word of mouth is counting on untrained marketers to decide your values and tell others about you. It also requires 100 percent customer satisfaction, which is impossible to sustain. It's also hard to generate or measure by the business. It's possible to build an incredible reputation and brand awareness, so word does spread through word of mouth. However, it can be as much of a liability as an opportunity. I wish you luck with word of mouth but never count on it.

Social media is a great tool. I won't delve deep into it as I did in Chapter 7, but if you want to leverage social media marketing, I have some helpful tips.

First, check your grammar. You'll look unprofessional if you have spelling errors or typos. You can use a browser extension like Grammarly for free that will catch the vast majority of your mistakes.

Next, use something to grab attention. Polls, videos, and photos are great ways to get your potential customers to pay attention. If you use a photo, choose one that catches your attention. People especially like seeing people and animals in photos. And food: Don't forget the food.

Be aware of the Facebook "algorithms." When you post to your Facebook page, it typically goes to a mere fraction of your followers, and their interaction with the post determines how many times Facebook will end up sharing it with others. Facebook is in the business of keeping users engaged, so it won't share boring posts with many people without someone paying for them to be shared more.

How many social media followers does your business page have? If it's just a few, you'll need to work to grow your followers or boost your posts, so they are seen. If 100 percent of your followers see your post, but you only have 12 followers, your marketing will not reach far. Make sure your efforts are worthwhile. What I love about social media is, when someone follows your page, they have agreed to let you market to them. For free. Forever. The responsibility is on you to keep them engaged so they like, click, comment, and share, so Facebook continues showing them your messages.

Email marketing is exceptionally powerful. It takes work to get it established and working. First, you HAVE to use a service that allows subscribers to unsubscribe with the click of a button, or you're violating a law and subject to consequences. The two most popular email channels are Mail Chimp and Constant Contact. Both are easy drag-and-drop platforms to set up for businesses sending emails.

In my personal experience, Constant Contact is a little more user-friendly while Mail Chimp is more affordable and has more advanced tools. With Mail Chimp, you can have a free account with less than 5000 subscribers. There are many other good options as well such as SendInBlue and MailerLite. Especially if you're on a free tier, I'm not going to split hairs on recommending which.

When you send emails, timing is important. You want your recipients to act now. If you send out your newsletter too early or too late, you can lose potential sales. You want to make it easy for your customers to do what you want them to do. If you want them to go to your website, provide the link to that specific site. If you want them to save a date, give them all the information they need. Don't make them work because most won't. Do the work for them, and you'll get the best results.

With email marketing, you need to acquire customers' email addresses. There are a lot of ways to do this. You can have a raffle for a prize that requires them to provide an email address and opt into your newsletter. You can have a signup form on your website that registers users to your list. You can rent or buy an email list.

I will say from experience that I have had success with email marketing, especially for live events. And every time I send out an email newsletter for my business, I see an immediate spike in my website traffic. Email marketing works if you have the email addresses of people who are capable of buying your products or services. It works, especially if you make it easy for them to buy from you.

Guerilla marketing is another low-cost marketing option that is effective. It capitalizes on the "wow" factor. A beautiful example of this took place in Australia when theaters released the new *It* movie. They had single red balloons tied to high-visibility sewage drains around the city. People were familiar with the balloon if they'd seen the movie's trailer, so the real-life balloons were an effective reminder to buy a ticket.

It is wonderful when marketing is that easy, affordable, and memorable, but less imaginative endeavors can be highly effective. For example, a new sandwich shop can take trays of "fun-sized" sandwiches to local businesses. Everyone loves free food, so it won't likely be rejected or ignored.

The only barriers to guerilla marketing are creativity and effort. It's a great way to have fun with your brand, reach new customers, and make lasting impressions.

If you are out there providing your services to the community at large, make sure you're taking advantage of your marketing opportunities:

- Does your van have signage on it?
- Is there a sign in your customer's yard where you're working?
- Does your shirt have your business name on it?
- Can you give a gymnast of the month award and have them put a sign in their yard for a month advertising your business?
- Can you sell or give away t-shirts that feature your business name and do marketing legwork on your behalf?

Take advantage of the easy wins for the most impact. These activities are low-money and low-time commitment. That's a win-win!

One way that is extremely powerful to spread the word about your business is networking. When you're shaking hands with people on the streets, you are having one-to-one conversations, which takes considerable time to reach the masses. In strategic networking events, you can reach one-to-many, which is more of a sweet spot for optimizing the time to grow awareness of your business.

I'd recommend asking a connected business person or your local chamber of commerce what opportunities exist in your area for networking. Many marketing approaches are "shotgun" approaches that go out in many directions. With networking, you have the opportunity to target your most likely new customers and give them the information they need to choose your business.

I suggest starting with your customer in mind. What does your customer look like? At which networking events are they likely to attend? That's where you need to be. Consider trade shows, flea markets, and farmers' markets. There are many different kinds of gatherings of people that are ripe with opportunities. The key thing to remember is that many people are there to socialize and the cherry on top is networking. Try to find a genuine connection with them, and they'll remember you and your business.

Obviously, advertising is part of marketing. It is wonderful, but it isn't free. The previous marketing solutions were free or low-cost. Many of them were trading time, energy, and a little money in exchange for boosting your brand's awareness. Advertising is trading money and a little time in exchange for brand awareness.

There are many different advertising venues. Digital marketing, billboards, radio, TV, newspapers, magazines, and a thousand other little opportunities that range from your name on kids' sports jerseys to an airplane dragging behind a banner with your phone number on it. There are millions of other opportunities. To find out which one will work best for you, ask yourself two questions:

- Who are my customers?
- Where am I likely to find them?

If you're looking for seniors, the newspaper is a good bet. If you have a restaurant right off the highway, a properly placed billboard could be a game-changer.

Unless the situation dictates otherwise, my go-to for budget advertising leans toward digital advertising. It's a cost-effective bang for the buck. What I love about digital ads is you can measure them, see the results, and narrow down who sees them with laser precision. The cost is less than many of the other advertising channels.

If none of the other marketing channels seems to be the ideal opportunity for your business, digital marketing is always a great go-to channel. This can be done through several different platforms. In my opinion, ads on social media are a little easier to place than on search engines like Google. To advertise on Meta (the owner of Facebook and Instagram), you can go to business.facebook.com to the Business Manager suite and get ads going there.

Running campaigns on Google Adwords is a little trickier. Google seems pretty unforgiving and offers little to no support if you need help.

The simpler way to do both is to just boost posts. When you post to social media, you send your message to a percentage of those who follow your social media account. The average recipient is 2 percent of your following the last time I checked. When the post receives "meaningful interactions," such as likes, comments, and shares, it goes to more. If you want a greater reach than this, there is a "pay to play" model called boosting that allows you to decide which kinds of followers you'd like to reach, and it will go to that kind of people. You can target locations, demographics, behaviors, and more.

It still follows the "algorithm," so the more meaningful interactions it receives, the greater the reach it will achieve. However, boosting posts doesn't provide as much targeting freedom as the ad manager portals allow.

All businesses need some form of advertising. Once you've figured out who your ideal audience is, decide where you can reach them, and then seek them out. Know what your marketing budget is, and find the best way to invest the money to get the best return. You might need to experiment to get the results you want.

You also might consider hiring a marketing agency to assist with these decisions and make recommendations. Sometimes, it's worth paying for expert advice.

Chapter 17

Growing

I have a friend who amassed several businesses and a large real estate and investment portfolio in a short time. He also started on a shoestring budget and used every resource available to him along with a whole lot of gumption to grow his empire brick by brick. What he has done is impressive, yet also scary to me. I become a scaredy-cat when my financial obligations increase. The what-ifs play in my head.

He's doing well for himself, obviously, but he's leveraged his resources to get the largest possible yield out of them. I asked him one day how he had enough confidence to take on that much debt and obligation for the empire he's growing. I often think about the advice he shared:

> "If you hire an employee, for say, $50,000 per year, you don't have to pay them $50,000 all at once. You only have to pay them for that month. Do you have enough resources to make payroll that month? And then the next month you do it again. When you sign

on to mortgages for investment properties, you don't have to obsess over the big number, just as long as you have enough resources to make each individual payment. As long as every investment is a good decision, it will work out. And if it doesn't, you will figure it out when the time comes. No great reward comes without great effort and great risk."

This book isn't about growing a shoestring side hustle. This book is about growing a *Shoestring Empire*. Empires are not built overnight and are not for the faint of heart. If it were easy, everyone would do it. Empires take strategy, resources, blood, sweat, and tears. The questions you have to ask yourself are:

- Are you all in?
- Do you believe in your business so much you're willing to take the risk?
- Could you live with knowing you didn't give it your all?

Mediocrity is perfectly acceptable. You can proceed with your business just the same. But if your answer is you can't live without trying, what is standing between you and your empire? For me, that answer was fear. And I refuse to let fear win.

To build your empire, you need to be able to add scale:

- Where is the bottleneck in your business?
- Is there a certain part of your business that you have inadequate manpower to operate?
- Inadequate equipment?
- Inadequate inventory?

I've seen a lot of businesses throw money at problems they don't fully understand and expect to fix the problem. This often results in a lot of money spent on technology that might not be helpful. You can't fix the issue until you understand what the issue is. If you're not an expert on the problem, become one or hire one.

The trick isn't spending money.

The trick is spending money well.

When you are ready to hire an employee, you need to be clear on this: Is this employee going to make you money or cost you money? They are making you money if:

- They are actually fulfilling customer orders.
- You are billing for their time.
- They are selling your products.
- They are producing products that you can sell at a profit.

When you hire money-making employees, if they are hired and managed well, they make your business more profitable. A lot of things have to be done right to monetize their services, but hiring money-making employees is often a smart thing to do.

On the other hand, some employees are expenses. These employees often fill the roles of quality assurance, middle management, human resources, and secretaries, and they cost you money. Please don't mistake the word "expense" for "worthless" or "bad," but you need to be aware that they are an expense that will offset your profits. These people are important and can make or break your business, but when you are starting out with limited resources, hiring employees who are not profit-making should be done with caution. It may be the best thing to do, but make sure you think it through.

I have a friend who had a t-shirt business and made all of the t-shirts herself. She had to turn down a few orders because she couldn't fulfill them. She was scared to add an extra employee to help make t-shirts because she didn't currently have enough orders to occupy two people's time. She finally decided to take the plunge and hired an employee. She was able to spend some time promoting her business, and sooner than expected, she had to hire another employee to keep up with the demand.

Adding money-making employees, if managed well, makes you more money. Adding headcount, pieces of equipment, new offerings, and more are all wonderful things and definitely a step in the right direction for growing your business. But refer back to Chapter 13 on when to spend and make sure you're making the best decisions. High overhead expenses reduce profits. Empires have high overheads. It's not a bad thing. It's a balancing act of how to get where you need to go with the least expenses. It's a chess game of deciding when to spend and when to sacrifice.

You Can Do It

Chapter 18
Worth it all

Since owning my own business, I've worked harder than I ever have before. Not only that, but in the first year or so, I made less money than I had ever made in my professional life. I thought working for others and managing departments was stressful, but it's a whole new kind of stress knowing the buck absolutely stops with me.

Cashflow in a new business was something I had never dealt with. A customer has promised you money, and maybe the check is really in the mail, but you have bills to pay today. You also worry about any legal issues that arise. That's the stress of a business owner. It's not the same as a manager's stress.

But is it worth it?

It may not be worth it to everyone. I was talking to a friend who had a stroke while dealing with the stress of owning her own business. I've talked to entrepreneurs who have grown distant from their families while focusing single-mindedly on their businesses. I have talked to business owners that have discovered that they love doing what they do, but they don't like managing the day-to-day responsibilities of owning a business. If any of those describe you, it doesn't mean you're incapable of owning your own business. But it may not be worth the sacrifices.

But for me?

I love the fact that when I kill myself to make a deadline or reach a milestone, it's for something that matters. I know I'm growing my empire and my current challenges are obstacles to overcome on my journey to success.

As an entrepreneur, I love that I can have an amazing new idea, make the decision (or not) to move forward with it, and then profit from its success.

As a leader, I love that I can recognize, appreciate, and reward my employees according to their contributions and talents.

As a mom, I love that I can arrange my schedule around my kids' gymnastics and archery meets with no questions asked.

As a humanitarian, I love that I can make decisions to support worthwhile causes as I'm able.

As a woman, I love that I can hire and pay women fairly and not fall into the nationwide statistics.

For me, this makes the long nights and the stressful hiccups all worthwhile.

You already have what it takes to launch a successful business. People far dumber than I am have successful businesses. People have launched empires with far less starting capital than I had. People lazier than I am have grown multi-million dollar organizations. If they can do it, so can I, and so can you. It's never easy, and it's never free, but it's certainly possible.

So, is it worth it for you?

The long hours?

The risk?

The stress?

Only you can make that determination. You need to figure out your "WHY?" and hold on to that. When the going gets tough, reflect on it. When you're tired and your motivation falters, go back to your "WHY?" When you're planning your strategies and charting your next move, think about it. And when you're more successful than you ever imagined, remember it then too.

I fear regret more than I fear failure. That's my mantra. I say it to myself every single day. It isn't always true, but I strive for it to be true. I feel confident that I could reflect back on my life on my deathbed and make peace with a business failure. I don't know that I could make peace with never mustering up the courage to try.

You have the tools. Go and do awesome things! Make up your mind that you are going to do it, and then do it. Relentlessly pursue your dreams. Don't apologize for your hustle. Own your shortcomings and then find a way to overcome them.

You CAN build an empire. And your current lack of financial resources is just one thing that you have the tools to eliminate.

Go forward, and grow your *Shoestring Empire*.

Note to reader

If you would like to review some of the resources mentioned in this book, go to https://shoestringempire.com for information, links, and additional ideas along with the free downloadable workbook. If you are inspired by this book to move forward on your business journey, we'd love for you to share your story on the website as well.

Sources

https://www.pewresearch.org/internet/fact-sheet/social-media/?menuItem=81867c91-92ad-45b8-a964-a2a894f873ef

https://blog.hubspot.com/blog/tabid/6307/bid/10322/the-ultimate-list-50-local-business-directories.aspx

https://blog.hootsuite.com/youtube-stats-marketers/

https://www.socialmediaexaminer.com/4-ways-to-use-tiktok-business/

https://www.businessnewsdaily.com/9860-snapchat-for-business.html

https://legaljobs.io/blog/divorce-rate-in-america/

https://www.bdc.ca/en/articles-tools/marketing-sales-export/marketing/what-average-marketing-budget-for-small-business#:~:text=In%20the%20simplest%20terms%2C%20your,%E2%80%94between%205%20and%2010%25.

https://www.fundera.com/blog/sba-definition-of-small-business

https://www.fastcapital360.com/blog/free-legal-advice/

Made in the USA
Columbia, SC
05 June 2025